TWO SOULS
ONE REFLECTION

Two Souls One Reflection

An Expression of Love, Intimacy, and Affection in Romantic Relationships

MUHAMMAD HASSAN RAZA

RESOURCE *Publications* • Eugene, Oregon

TWO SOULS ONE REFLECTION
An Expression of Love, Intimacy, and Affection in Romantic Relationships

Copyright © 2024 Muhammad Hassan Raza. All rights reserved. Except for brief quotations in critical publications or reviews, no part of this book may be reproduced in any manner without prior written permission from the publisher. Write: Permissions, Wipf and Stock Publishers, 199 W. 8th Ave., Suite 3, Eugene, OR 97401.

Resource Publications
An Imprint of Wipf and Stock Publishers
199 W. 8th Ave., Suite 3
Eugene, OR 97401

www.wipfandstock.com

PAPERBACK ISBN: 979-8-3852-0884-5
HARDCOVER ISBN: 979-8-3852-0885-2
EBOOK ISBN: 979-8-3852-0886-9

04/01/24

For questions or additional information about this book, please contact the author at twosoulsonereflection@gmail.com

I dedicate my book to my family which is as follows:

Zeenat Raza (My wife)
Hussain Raza (My older son)
Rasti Raza (My daughter)
Ali Raza (My younger son)

CONTENTS

Introduction	ix
1. Your Reflection	1
2. Two Souls One Reflection	2
3. You Are My Fortune	3
4. Feelings of Love	4
5. Two Hearts and Breeze	5
6. I Wish My Poetry Could	7
7. Love is Magic	8
8. Our Love and Relationship	9
9. Your Memories for Me	10
10. You are my Passion	11
11. Will Fall in Love with Me	13
12. My Life and Your Love	14
13. I Am Alone	16
14. You Are To Me	17
15. My Love and You	18
16. Days Were Spring	19

17. Love and Distance	21
18. Don't Make Excuses	22
19. Arrest Me in Your Love	23
20. My Feelings for You	24
21. You Don't Care of Me	25
22. Make a Promise with Me	26
23. I Make your Picture in my Heart	27
24. Who Are We To Each Other?	28
25. When You Say Goodbye	29
26. I Wish this Could Happen	30
27. I And My Love	32
28. My Request for You	33
29. Our Friendship and Intimacy	34
30. I Wish I Could Cry	35
31. A Fight with Night	36
32. Faces Shine	38
33. You Are my Universe	40
34. When I Sing	41
35. Students' Voice for a Professor	44
The Author	47

INTRODUCTION

THIS POETRY BOOK INCLUDES poems of various kinds. This book is a unique expression of intimacy and love in romantic relationships. This book shares and promotes positive emotions and feelings of love relationships among its readers. It also presents tragedy of distance, conflict, challenges of romance, and misunderstanding in relationships and how both lovers feel and experience these situations in their romantic relationship. Hence, the book provides its readers with a variety of situations and imagination that they can feel and experience.

1. YOUR REFLECTION

Your reflection, night, and snow.
Strikes in body, my heart blows.

A Sun of your picture grows.
Thus, your reflection does not go.

Story of love in the flow.
I fell in love a decade ago.

Can anyone tell which path to go?
My heart cries, I injure my toes.

When she comes, her face glows.
I wish the day goes a bit slow.

My mind says go away, just go.
My heart says always shows.

So tired and hungry, but no one shows.
Can someone give me bread or dough?

Keep trying until you die or grow.
If you die, your body will flow.

My poems describe your solo.
No one comes in my words though.

While she looks at me with love.
She does not dare to say hello.

I miss you and the rainbow.
No one returns from there you know.

2. TWO SOULS ONE REFLECTION

You and I are two souls.
We are two parts of a whole.

We support each other's goals.
I feel like we are in full control.

We change our every day's roles.
It's impossible to live apart anymore.

My emotions go beyond the door.
When I kiss you, I want more and more.

You are my heart, and I am yours' for sure.
We are one reflection of two souls.

3. YOU ARE MY FORTUNE

I wish I could change my fortune.
You and I share a spoon.

We hold hands and fly balloons.
Our relationship stays in finetune.

Your beauty shines like a moon.
Your body smells like saffron.

We enjoy a beach at noon.
Dress maroon and shop in afternoon

Please come see me in June.
I miss our romance in the bedroom.

I wish fortune would come soon.
You bring joy and become my opportune.

4. FEELINGS OF LOVE

Love shows and hide.
It keeps people tight.

Feels magical in heart and mind.
Light, alright, and satisfied.

I follow you like a guide.
Crazy to see you on sight.

You will find as you decide.
It's a treasure that stays inside.

Sometimes it leaves people behind.
Sometimes it becomes their pride.

It's a journey that you take a ride.
Sadness and joy go side-by-side.

Love is emotions you feel inside.
It becomes a reality that can't be denied.

5. TWO HEARTS AND BREEZE

One day, I was alone.
Sitting at my home.
Scratching a stone.
On my own.

Suddenly, I felt a breeze.
Which made me pleased.
I pulled my sleeves.
Took a deep breathe.

I asked the breeze.
Whenever you leave.
And go to her street.
Touch her cheeks.
Bend on knees.
Tell her what I feel.

Describe my love.
Up and above.
It's been months.
Without her, life is tough.
This is not what I deserve.
She is my true love.

Please explain she is my life.
Stay always in my eyes.
Come, give me a surprise.
I do apologize.
Please don't say goodbyes.
My hopes are quite high.

After a while the breeze returns.
Tells me what she learned.
Explains how I am a dum.

She expects me to come.
Do what I never done.
A lesson I learned.
When you like someone.
Need to say from tongue.
Listening to the breeze was fun.
I felt that I won.

I am going as she is waiting.
I am glad she is still not dating.
Next morning flight I am taking.
The whole night, I will be waking.
Why waiting is irritating.
This experience is still fascinating.

I will hug her and kiss.
Then present my wish.
Without any miss.
I am going to fix.
If she accepts.
I will put a ring.
Together we sing.
Will have a drink.

6. I WISH MY POETRY COULD

Write a poem which talks to my heart.
Brings her in my dreams and thoughts.

Make me happy, so, my worry stops.
I become smart to compete with counterparts.

Prevent me from falling apart.
Hold me when I think and walk.

Decrease my sadness and pain of heart.
Fresh my soul, so, my life restarts.

My poetry describes what I watched.
Situations of distrust in which I caught.

When you ignored, I cried so hard.
It broke my heart in so many parts.

When you left, my life became a fault.
Please return and become my sweetheart.

7. LOVE IS MAGIC

I feel love is like magic.
It is hidden but feels exotic.

People's intimacy creates this fabric.
It is electric that makes you energetic.

Love accompanies with emotional traffic.
Joys, happiness, tears, and panic.

No one understands its logic.
When it comes to you automatic.

People like because of its aesthetic.
It is such feelings which make you erotic.

It is romantic, sweet, and dramatic.
It can be tragic and fully problematic.

Everyone gives up on this magic.
Love is neither static nor systematic.

I am proud to experience this magic.
No complaints, I don't need any credit.

8. OUR LOVE AND RELATIONSHIP

I am in love, feels like in your arrest.
This is not a regret, I feel blessed.

Your one look makes me impressed.
I feel it and become obsessed.

You are the best, which is a test.
I feel myself in a constant contest.

I dream of you each time I rest.
Don't get me up when I slept.

Our love makes us perfect.
Our relationship truly manifests.

I tell each time what I meant.
I love you with my heart and nothing instead.

9. YOUR MEMORIES FOR ME

Your remembrance makes your picture.
Without you, I can hear your whisper.

Your picture sings and my love triggers.
You become real and hold me in my inner.

Then I put a ring in your finger.
You smile and see it in a mirror.

I kiss you and look at your figure.
Our meeting becomes a thriller.

Your reflection gets bigger and bigger.
It feels real, not a sculpture.

Your memories work like a filler.
Makes me richer, I feel like a winner.

When my sorrow gets darker.
Your memories shine and become a healer.

10. YOU ARE MY PASSION

My love is passion.
Passion is emotions.
Seeking for sensation
Feeling a connection.

I wish you and me.
Enjoy coffee and tea.
Sit under the tree.
Stay beyond eighty.
You are my inspiration.
Feels like infatuation.
My love is passion.
Passion is emotions.
Seeking for sensation.
Feeling a connection.

We enjoy our time.
Some whiskey and wine.
Play socker over time.
Stand together and shine.
You are my attraction.
My love is passion.
Passion is emotions.
Seeking for sensation
Feeling a connection.

Let's promise to maintain it.
Do everything to sustain it.
Make love to entertain it.
It drains, we contain it.
Our love is our destination.
This is life and motivation.

My love is passion.
Passion is emotions.
Seeking for sensation
Feeling a connection.

We hold our hands.
Play guitar and bands.
Buy land and expand.
Go to beach get tend.
We are our fashion.
Satisfaction and compassion.
My love is passion.
Passion is emotions.
Seeking for sensation
Feeling a connection.

Let's romance all night.
Uncover some insights.
Make faces bright.
Touch, feel, and bite.
You are my reflection.
My attention and direction.
My love is passion.
Passion is emotions.
Seeking for sensation
Feeling a connection.

11. WILL FALL IN LOVE WITH ME

Spend some time to fall in love with me.
Read my rhyme to fall in love with me.

Become sleepless, restless, but committed.
Keep me prime to fall in love with me.

Think of love more than your life and soul.
Ready to climb to fall in love with me.

Show passion, empathy, and compassion.
Make you inclined to fall in love with me.

I passed every test of your love.
Stay lifetime to fall in love with me.

12. MY LIFE AND YOUR LOVE

Your love is my life.
It makes me alive.
Create a surprise.
I am ready to sacrifice.

When she describes.
The rhymes she writes.
I feel pride.
She goes sky high.
Everything looks bright.
I love that sight.

I literally fly.
My emotions go high.
Full of butterflies.
Feels quite satisfied.

You are my destination.
My life's inspiration.
I desire for our relation.
Let's continue our conversation.

You are who I believe.
Wish to touch your cheeks.
Walk down the streets.
Sit under the trees.

You give me a vibe.
My heart strikes.
When you smile.
My life is alright.

Let's live on the first floor.
Can't stay without you anymore.
Let's reunion and explore.
I admire you and adore.

You are my wealth.
My soul and breath.
My all-times success.
Am ready to confess.

I can be testified.
Ready to sacrifice.
Even I can die.
Please don't say goodbye.

You are my imagination.
A source of motivation.
Let's spend vacation.
Experience the situation.

My poems are in your name.
I don't have any shame.
You are what I explain.
Still so much remains.

Feel like I am crazy.
Keep thinking of you lately.
Practice it daily.
You are my lady.

Please become my pride.
Let's give it a try.
You will be satisfied.
I will make you, my bride.

13. I AM ALONE

I am alone.
Among plenty of stones.
No water in this zone.
Did I do something wrong?

No drink but stones.
Neither shelter, nor any home.
This place is unknown.
Feels like I still belong.

I feel no one welcomes.
There is no affection.
No respect and connection.
This is a time for reflection.
There is a lack of sincerity.
It is full of deception.

Don't be silly.
It's simply not your city.
Everyone is busy.
No time for whisky.
You shouldn't be guilty.
Don't expect any sympathy.
No friends but enemy
Better leave the city.

14. YOU ARE TO ME

Air flows and flowers bloom.
Forgive people, give them room.

She has a fragrance like perfume.
No one knows where she groomed.

Weather of love seems like fortune.
Make her bride and becomes a groom.

Her voice lightens my heart and soul.
She is a universe who I assume.

I enjoyed a coffee with her.
I adored a few noon and afternoon.

I feel you with me everywhere.
I find you in my lawn and bedroom.

Don't you remember the night before you left.
We ate sushi together with a spoon.

I hope you meet me soon.
I want to enjoy our honeymoon.

15. MY LOVE AND YOU

My stories were new but got old.
I loved the place where I stoned.

Last night when you showed.
I felt we never met as you unfold.

You changed yourself and rolled.
It felt like my joys got a hold.

You weren't like that anymore.
Or I was not wise before.

You always wished to ignore.
I always wanted some more.

All paths towards her are closed.
Feels like situations aren't controlled.

16. DAYS WERE SPRING

Days are spring.
We stand like strings.
Beautiful time.
Birds sing rhymes.

Green trees swing.
We cling.
My heart rings.
You are everything.

You are my dear.
Who I only care.
Change my atmosphere.
You and a beer.
Make me happy.
When we share.

You left fast.
My heart blasts.
Life changed and time passed.
I cried and people laughed.
Pleasant times became a past.
No one cared who I asked.

You are gone.
I am alone.
Neither text nor phone.
Why became unknown.
It's been quite long.
I couldn't sing a song.

Wish you could come here.
Make my dreams real.
I wait for you.
Stick like glue.
Without a clue.
Keep hopes and look through.

Eager to meet.
Hold a treat.
With sweets and meat.
In the same street.
Please reach.
Standing on my feet.
Check my heartbeat.
Without you.
My life is incomplete.

It's a request.
You are the best.
Please don't delete.
You do mistreat.
When you ignore.
I face defeat.
Please come.
Make my life complete.

17. LOVE AND DISTANCE

Love accompanies distance and glory.
Distance is a gift comes mandatory.

Don't come until I am alive.
Your arrival incompletes our love story

I find you in the darkness of my heart.
Your love gives me some auditory.

I was not eager to change my ways.
If you don't play distance obligatory.

Your distance took my whole life.
Dry, dark, my life became a bad story.

18. DON'T MAKE EXCUSES

Come, don't make excuses anymore.
I am not sure why you ignore.

O gentle wind, tell her, I am bored.
Been waiting for her at my door.

You haven't come, it's already four.
It happened many times before.

Please understand commitment is the core.
It hurts me and no one is for cure.

Poetry is not just words to adore.
It is an expression of my soul.

I look behind to repair and secure.
It seems like our relationship is premature.

Feelings and emotions are to explore.
When you love, then they pour.

When I feel empty, and I am bored.
See your pictures when open my drawer.

Your memories make me cry and roar.
In my heart and mind, they are stored.

I am waiting, holding your Dior.
I love you; my feelings are pure.

19. ARREST ME IN YOUR LOVE

Oh beloved, arrest me in your love.
Waiting for your lips, give me a hug.

Your kiss is my drink which is all above.
Keep giving me this drug for ever enough.

Let me tell you that you are my crush.
You are my heart, mind, all my worth.

I dream of you what I deserve.
When I dream of you, don't wake me up.

Approve my love if you are brave enough.
Stop making my life rough and tough.

I keep your love up and above.
But you don't care enough about my stuff.

20. MY FEELINGS FOR YOU

We were like friends who don't date.
Though we were close, but never intimate.

I appreciate you and admit that you are great.
Your face demonstrates, and there is no debate.

Your beauty was beyond glory and praise.
I always wished you were my mate.

My heartbeat increases when we separate.
It's hard to elaborate that I can't articulate.

What should I do to compensate?
That you relate with me and celebrate.

If you don't come, tell me, and just communicate.
I expect you be straight, but you manipulate.

You are unpredictable, it is hard to anticipate.
I arrived on time, but you still consider me late.

I don't have intimacy with you, how can I create.
When I write my love story, I struggle to celebrate.

People are fortune who were your mate.
A state which I can't elaborate.

21. YOU DON'T CARE OF ME

People don't do this when they love.
If you love me, show me your love.

You are in a rush without saying much.
You are my crush; you don't care enough.

Your such treatment, I don't deserve.
I believe this is not what I worth.

Love needs expression, which is tough.
You need to talk, up and above.

My poetry shows that life is rough.
Your love shows, it is more than enough.

I am leaving but you don't care this stuff.
No laugh and talk, nothing to discuss.

I wish you love me like once.
You are my addiction; I take you like drugs.

22. MAKE A PROMISE WITH ME

Promise that in any situation, you will not cry.
Whatever happens, avoid tears in your eyes.

I agree that the storms are sky-high.
Promise that you will not say good-bye.

People are not happy when we meet.
Promise what they say, you will not comply.

If these storms separate us today.
Promise that you keep hope and try.

I know you made yourself quite busy.
Promise when have time, you will come by.

Know that I always trust you.
Promise you stay in love and will not deny.

23. I MAKE YOUR PICTURE IN MY HEART

I make your picture in my heart.
Which does not let me stay apart.

This art brings you into my thoughts.
Makes me think, you are my sweetheart.

Excitement and reactions begin to start.
My body moves towards your parts.

When I worry and want to depart.
Your picture stops me from tearing apart.

Is it you or a piece of art?
It surprises me for the most part.

My worry stops when your picture talks.
It feels real and makes me smart.

24. WHO ARE WE TO EACH OTHER?

If I am not wrong.
You are unknown.
I am alone.
You are your own.
Empty my life.
Full of stones.
Nothing between us.
Which makes us strong.
Sadness and distance.
You chose such zone.

I came by.
You were not home.
Tried to communicate.
You never picked up the phone.
Our relationship didn't work.
No one was wrong.

In our relationship.
Nothing grown.
We are two walls.
Not a home.
We lived together.
But still alone.

Let's break-up without too long.
Enjoy our life before it's gone.
Don't prove each other wrong.
Find someone who likes to sing songs.
Who can walk along.
About whom we feel strong.
Let's support and not date anymore.
It's a relationship none of us belongs.

25. WHEN YOU SAY GOODBYE

When you say goodbye, my eyes cry.
You are so dry; can you tell me why?

I am standing in the desert to testify.
I need water, supplies, or I will die.

It's all dry and above the sky.
I tried but no sleep in my eye.

Look at my condition, hey guy.
Come, fly, meet me to satisfy.

No air, no birds, and no flies.
Which solution should I apply?

I am sad with tears and sigh.
I wish I could have toys like butterflies.

Though you are alone but think high.
It is a reality that you can't deny.

26. I WISH THIS COULD HAPPEN

I wish this could happen.
You come to my home.
Walk long in my zone.
With a smile.
Come along.

I wish this could happen.
My heart used to sing.
You changed everything.
I feel nothing like spring.
My mood swings.
My heart forgot to ring.
Such charm and joy.
How could I bring?

I wish this could happen.
You come back.
Blossom flowers.
Speak louder.
Enlighten my inner.
Bright the outer.

You started arguments.
It was unfortunate.
I tried to coordinate.
You didn't feel pertinent.
I shared my feelings.
You made me irrelevant.

It was our love story.
We wrote it with glory.
You forgot our commitment.

And left me slowly.
It was a tragedy.
Revealed your duality.

I wish this could happen.
You think what you did.
Acknowledge and admit.
Forget everything.
Come back and sing.
Hold hands and swim.
We feel touch and skin.
I wish this could happen.
I wish this could happen.

27. I AND MY LOVE

I express my love to only one.
My love story is not for everyone.

People use gifts and symbols.
I express love with my tongue.

Careful before you think and experience it.
You feel undone, and never won.

My family laughs wholeheartedly at me.
They say, I love you, but you have fun.

Look into my eyes and listen.
A constant cry feels like just begun.

28. MY REQUEST FOR YOU

I feel blessed.
My friend is the best.
Without whom, I feel unrest.
I am quite obsessed.

She is my darling.
My life's charming.
We get up each morning.
Talking and walking.
Sit together, keep watching.
Hold hands for dancing.

She is my beloved.
Who I love.
She stays in my heart.
We build trust.
I want to touch.
I love her so much.

You are my joy.
Remains a bit shy.
You are who I rely.
Always shine in my eyes.

Please stay for life.
Become my wife.
Without you, I will die.
Your company makes me alive.

29. OUR FRIENDSHIP AND INTIMACY

I am so thirsty.
But you still show mercy.
We share ourselves with.
Our friendship is worthy.

You are my motivation.
My heart and foundation
I know you are there.
Will be with me in any situation.

We touch and feel.
Kiss, hug, and reveal.
Enjoy eating meals.
Walk like a wheel.

You are my proud.
Nothing that sound.
Loud and clear.
We make a strong bond.

Let's make an agreement.
We will show commitment.
Overtime, be consistent.
Will gain fulfilment.

Our friendship and intimacy.
Give us strength and efficacy.
We should hold it carefully.
Enjoy, celebrate it gracefully.

30. I WISH I COULD CRY

I wish I could cry.
But I can't, I don't lie.

When you leave me alone and say goodbye.
My body burns why I don't dye.

I look at the sky with my mouth dry.
I try to fly which is too high.

My eyes lie and my heart denies.
I feel this is the time to testify.

I send you messages through a butterfly.
This is the mode for me to rely.

I shine when you reply.
Come and show up from sky.

Give me a smile but stay shy.
This works like a blood supply.

There are no gifts that we buy.
We play with each other like a toy.

Then you leave and say goodbye.
It is time for me to die.

I don't dye but try to cry.
I can't, I wish I could cry.

31. A FIGHT WITH NIGHT

How long will this night go?
Stop hurting my heart and toe?

Tired my eyes, tears flow.
Though my face still glows.

The night moves a bit slow.
I cry, my worries grow.

It's all dark with shadow.
When morning comes, I don't know.

Inside quiet and outside snow.
Not sure, who I say hello.

Neither a moon, nor rainbow.
Looking at sky, grabbing a pillow.

Shadows are running on my patio.
Neither any birds, nor thirsty crow.

It's all real up and below.
Neither a dream nor TV show.

A fear with cry that grows.
The night persists which doesn't go.

I am all alone and solo.
It all dark, nowhere to go?

This night stays, will not go.
Feels like it will further grow.

I am determined to fight with shadow.
I keep hope to through it below.

The day comes, night will go.
Will see birds flying in a row.

It's quite hard and tough though.
Tonight, will pass, tomorrow will show.

Tears will stop, my face glows.
Will enjoy snow and wait for rainbow.

Exciting life with butter and dough.
Watching TV and listen to Radio.

Friends, drive, and music with flow.
Walmart, ShopRite, shopping Cosco.

I will beat this night and shadow.
It is a fight that I owe.

32. FACES SHINE

Some faces shine.
Seems like mine.
Stay in your heart.
Feels right and fine.

When sadness climbs.
No one shares wine.
Those faces show that time.
Smile and shine
Makes you a valentine.
Read a rhyme.
Your time becomes prime.

Those faces are rare.
They care and become fair.
Feels like you want to share.
Enjoy a bear and cheer.
You know they are aware.
That's why you declare.
Sitting on a chair.
Ready to go anywhere.

If you eager to find.
Don't go behind.
Show pride and be kind.
Connect and intertwined.
Share, reveal, and rewind.
Enlighten your heart and mind.

They will come to you.
When they appear, no clue.
Need to keep an open view.

Not a lot, will see a few.
Keep a goal and pursue.
Surely you will be through.

They don't come in vain.
Bring joy or strain.
Be ready for pain.
It's a game, shouldn't complain.
Use brain and try again.
Success and failure stay the same.
If they shine, be happy, you gain.
If they strain, no shame, no blame.
Faces shine, they come in a chain.
Read those faces, be ready to explain.
Choose the ones who gain, not drain.
It's still a game and chances remain.

33. YOU ARE MY UNIVERSE

Are you a human, or a universe?
Priceless you are, beyond any worth.

My love is for you, you are my love.
I am surprised at what you deserve.

Are you a book, or a few words?
Freshness of morning, or a pair of pearls.

Are you a prize, or a tough serve.
Course of life, a few moments of converse.

Are you an angle, divine, or a verse?
Feelings of heart, mind, or a nerve.

Are you a music, or hearing I preserve?
Sun's light, moon, or rain on earth.

Are you a spirit, soul, or love?
Hatred of life, worse, or adverse.

Are you a star, planet, or a world.
Not sure, but you are my universe.

34. WHEN I SING

When I sing
Something inside rings.
Feel you touch my chin.
Kiss my skin.
How long it's been.
Nothing in between.

I am not evergreen.
Why create such scenes.
I am just a teen.
Not sure what that means.
Stop ruing my dreams.
Let's make something.
Become a team.
When I sing
Something inside rings

When leaves fall.
I go to a bar.
Keep myself far.
My mind still recalls.
Our memories so far.
Which are my all.
You were my superstar.
Sitting in the car.
Going to a mall.
Playing baseball.
Eating pizza on a walk.
Watching pieces of art.
Sharing feelings and thoughts.
Collecting leaves in a jar.
Do you remember that fall?

Why became apart.
Made our life so hard.
Let's be smart.
Do your part.
Shine like a star.
Remain sweethearts.
I adore what you bring.
You are my everything.
It feels like spring.
When I sing.

You make me satisfied.
I cry when you deny.
Why are you so shy?
Why don't you reply?
Stop saying goodbye.
My life becomes dry.
Promise I don't lie.
Please understand and rely.
Otherwise, I will die.
Without you, there is no tie.
Your arrival brings butterflies.
Look into my eyes.
Will fly sky high.
We can begin.
Stay within.
Make a string.
Together we win.
It feels like spring.
When I sing.

Let's have fun.
Shine like Sun.
Together we run.
Will keep us young.

Yours mine and none.
Don't wait, please come.
Touch my chin.
Kiss my skin.
It feels like spring.
When I sing.

35. STUDENTS' VOICE FOR A PROFESSOR

Hey professor, listen to us.
Give us a break, please don't rush.
Need some time to absorb the stuff.
Let us catch up and not lose enough.

We know, we need a pass.
Although, a mess, it's a class.
How you started, what it was.
It feels tough, without any pause.

We know you need to talk.
You have too much in stock.
It is class, we came to ask.
It helps if you look at the clock.

We like to share and engage.
Don't want to sit in a cage.
We need expression at this age.
It hurts when we feel disengaged.

We like you so much.
You give us education with real touch.
We promise to continue without being shut.
But you need to trust.

Can you do what we like.
Assuring you will not disappoint.
Will do our work right and bright.
Please listen to our voice.

Let's plan and begin.
Do our job and sing.

Work together and win.
Utilize strengths which are within.

We reflect and express our needs.
Please let us take the lead.
It's beneficial for us indeed.
We appreciate the way you teach.

Hey professor, experience, and feel.
This is our humble appeal.
We can recover and still heal.
If you make a good deal.

                                                           To be continued…...

THE AUTHOR

Dr. Raza is an Associate Professor at Missouri State University, Springfield, United States. He is a theorist and a methodologist. He is the author of a book called "The Multilevel Community Engagement Model: School, Community, Workplace Engagement and Service-Learning." He has been writing poetry and songs since he was in high school. He writes poetry in English and Urdu. In addition to writing poetry and songs, he also writes drama and film. After work, he likes to spend time with his family, which includes his spouse and three young children. He also likes to travel and visit new places to explore and enjoy.

www.ingramcontent.com/pod-product-compliance
Lightning Source LLC
Chambersburg PA
CBHW061257040426
42444CB00010B/2406